# Experiments
## with
# FORCES

Isabel Thomas

heinemann raintree

© 2016 Heinemann Raintree
an imprint of Capstone Global Library, LLC
Chicago, Illinois

To contact Capstone Global Library, please call
800-747-4992, or visit our website www.capstonepub.com

Edited by Holly Beaumont and Mandy Robbins
Designed by Steve Mead
Picture research by Jo Miller
Production by Helen McCreath
Originated by Capstone Global Library Ltd
Printed and bound in the USA by Corporate Graphics

19 18 17 16 15
10 9 8 7 6 5 4 3 2 1

Library of Congress Cataloging-in-Publication Data
Thomas, Isabel, 1979- author.
  Experiments with forces / Isabel Thomas.
    pages cm.—(Read and experiment)
  Summary: "Read and Experiment is an engaging series, in-
troducing children to scientific concepts. Explore the world of
forces with clear text, real-world examples and fun, safe step-
by-step experiments. This book brings the science of forces to
life, explaining the concepts and encouraging children to be
hands-on scientists."—Provided by publisher.
  Includes bibliographical references and index.
  ISBN 978-1-4109-7921-6 (hb)—ISBN 978-1-4109-7927-8 (pb)—
ISBN 978-1-4109-7938-4 (ebook)  1. Force and energy—
Experiments—Juvenile literature. 2.  Science projects—
Juvenile literature.  I. Title.

  QC73.4.T45 2016
  531.6078—dc23    2014041762

*This book has been officially leveled by using the F&P Text
Level Gradient™ Leveling System.*

Acknowledgements
We would like to thank the following for permission to repro-
duce photographs: Corbis: C. Devan, 16; Dreamstime: Jorg
Hackemann, cover (bottom); Getty Images: Image Source,
10; iStockphoto: curtis_creative, 22; Newscom: EPA/Diego
Azubel, 21, Itar-Tass Photos, 5, Novastock Stock Connection
Worldwide, 27; Shutterstock: 2xSamara.com, 7, Anastaslia
Markus, 17; U.S. Navy photo by SKC Michael Murphy, 15
(bottom)

All other photographs were created at Capstone Studio by
Karon Dubke.

We would like to thank Patrick O'Mahony for his invaluable
help in the preparation of this book.

Every effort has been made to contact copyright holders
of material reproduced in this book. Any omissions will be
rectified in subsequent printings if notice is given to the
publisher.

All the internet addresses (URLs) given in this book were valid
at the time of going to press. However, due to the dynamic
nature of the internet, some addresses may have changed, or
sites may have changed or ceased to exist since publication.
While the author and publisher regret any inconvenience this
may cause readers, no responsibility for any such changes can
be accepted by either the author or the publisher.

The publisher and author disclaim, to the maximum extent
possible, all liability for any accidents, injuries, or losses that
may occur as a result of the information or instructions in
this book.

**Safety instructions for adult helper**
The experiments in this book should be planned and carried out with adult supervision. Certain steps should
**only** be carried out by an adult, such as punching holes with a screwdriver (page 8) – these are indicated in
the text. Look out for these signs, and always follow the instructions carefully.

# Contents

Some words are shown in bold, **like this**. You can find out what they mean by looking in the glossary.

# Why Experiment?

Why does falling down hurt when sitting down doesn't?

Why do huge ships float but tiny paperclips sink?

You can be a scientist by asking questions about the world and using experiments to help find the answers.

Follow these steps to work like a scientist:

Ask a question.

↓

Come up with an idea to test.

↓

Plan an experiment.

↓

What will you change?
What will you keep the same?
What will you measure?

↓

Make a **prediction**.

↓

**Observe** carefully.

↓

Work out what the results mean.

↓

Answer the question!

Scientists ask questions like these. They work out the answers using **scientific inquiry**—and the really fun part is the **experiments**!

An experiment is a test that has been carefully planned to answer a question.

The experiments in this book will help you to find out more about **forces** and how they affect everything we do.

## IS IT A FAIR TEST?

Most experiments involve changing something to see what happens. Make sure you only change one **variable** at a time. Then you will know that the variable you are testing is what made the difference. This is called a fair test.

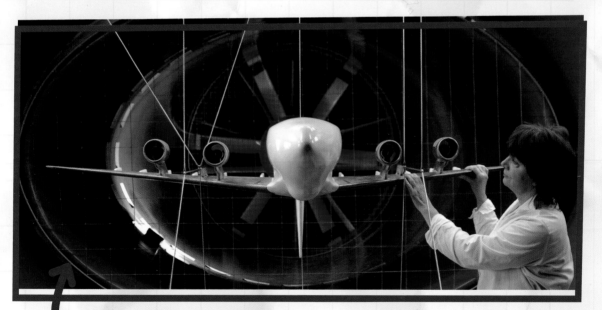

Get your eyes, ears, nose, and hands ready! You'll need to observe your experiments carefully and record what you see, hear, smell, and feel.

**WARNING!** Ask an adult to help you plan and carry out each experiment. Follow the instructions carefully. If you see these signs, you will need to take extra care or ask for adult help.

# What Is a Force?

**Forces** are pushes or pulls. We can't see forces, but we can see their effects. It's forces that make things start moving, stop moving, speed up, slow down, change direction, or change shape.

Forces are around us all the time. A force called gravity pulls a balloon towards the ground if you drop it. Air inside pushes on the walls of the balloon, keeping it inflated. Tapping, holding, or blowing the balloon all produce forces.

## SEE THE SCIENCE ⬇

Blow up and tie a balloon. Use forces to make it start moving, stop moving, change direction, and change shape. How many different ways can you push or pull the balloon?

Push down on a spring and you can feel it pushing back. The harder you push, the harder the spring pushes back. The same happens when you push against a wall. The tiny particles making up the wall push back to stop themselves being squeezed together. The harder you push, the harder they push back.

## Pushing Back

Forces come in pairs. When you push or pull a wall, the wall pushes or pulls back just as hard, in the **opposite** direction. If the wall wasn't pushing back, it would fall over!

The push of the ground is easy to feel when you fall down—ouch!

# Make Your Own Engine

This machine is known as Hero's engine. It was invented more than 2,000 years ago. Build it, and use it to show that **forces** come in pairs.

## Equipment

- Empty juice carton (the taller, the better)
- Screwdriver
- Jug and water
- 3-foot (1-meter) length of yarn

## Method

1. Ask an adult to make a small hole near the bottom corner of the carton and two small holes at the top.

2. Thread the yarn through the holes at the top to make a long handle.

**Predict**: What will happen when you fill the carton with water?

**3** Fill the carton with water and use the handle to lift it off the ground. What happens? Record your **observations**.

**4** Ask an adult to help you make a second hole in the **opposite** corner. Test the engine again.

Predict: What will happen if you make more holes?

⚠ Work outdoors or hold the carton over a bath!

## Conclusion

The force of gravity makes water shoot out of the holes in the carton. Forces always come in pairs, so a force is also pushing back on the carton in the opposite direction. This pushing force makes the carton spin around. When you make more holes, more water escapes, and the pushing force is bigger. The carton spins faster.

# Balanced or Unbalanced?

**Forces** (pushes and pulls) can make objects move. They can also make objects stay still.

## Balanced Forces

The forces on the doll are **balanced**. They are the same size but pulling the doll in **opposite** directions. They cancel each other out, so the doll stays still.

We can't see forces, but we can use arrows to show their size and direction.

You can tell if the forces on an object are balanced—they will not change how the object moves:

- If the object is still, it will stay still (for example, the doll in the picture).
- If the object is moving, it will keep moving in the same direction. It will not speed up or slow down (for example, a car traveling at one speed along a motorway).

## SEE THE SCIENCE ⬎

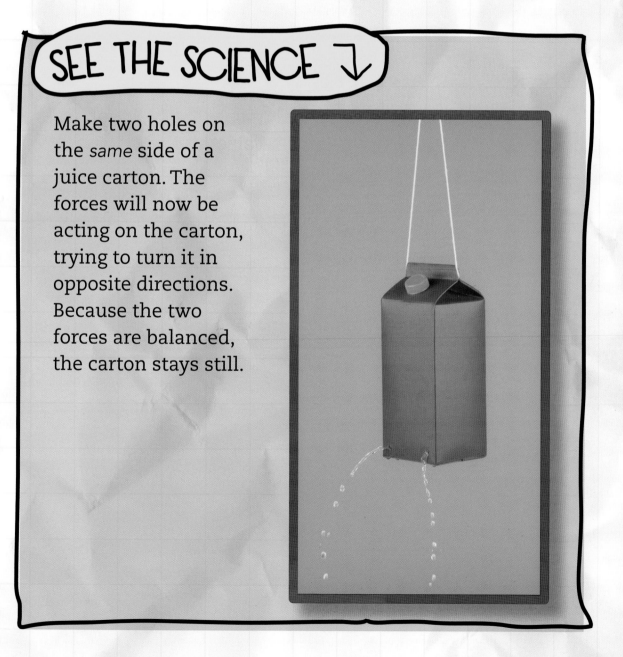

Make two holes on the *same* side of a juice carton. The forces will now be acting on the carton, trying to turn it in opposite directions. Because the two forces are balanced, the carton stays still.

# SEE THE SCIENCE ↴

If you push equally hard in **opposite** directions, the boat does not move, no matter how hard you push. The forces are **balanced**. Only unbalanced forces change the way an object moves, as with the rubber duck below.

# Submarine Captain

Can you balance the forces on a submarine so that it hovers underwater?

## Equipment

- Small plastic bottle with a lid
- Small beads
- Large glass bowl, jug, or vase
- Water

## Method

1  The plastic bottle is your submarine. Start by making it float on the surface of the water. Did you have to add anything to the bottle? Record what you did to make the submarine float.

| Aim | What I did |
|-----|-----------|
| Float on the surface | |
| Sink to the bottom | |
| Hover in the middle | |

Draw a table to record what you did.

**2** Now use beads to sink the submarine. Record what you did.

**3** Finally, try to make the submarine hover in the middle of the container. It must not touch the surface of the water or the bottom or sides of the bottle. Record what you did to make this happen.

## Conclusion

When you put an object into water, it pushes some of the water out of its way. The water pushes back. This is called **buoyancy** (or upthrust), and it pushes an object upwards.

Did you find that a bottle filled with air floats but the same bottle filled with objects sinks? The bottle is the same size each time but adding beads changes its weight and **density**.

When the submarine's weight is greater than the buoyancy, the submarine sinks. This happens when the density of the submarine becomes greater than the density of water. The submarine stops when it hits the bottom. The upward push of the bowl, jug, or vase **balances** the downward push of the submarine.

If the submarine's weight and the buoyancy are balanced, the submarine will hover in the water. This happens when the density of the submarine is exactly the same as the density of water.

weight due to gravity

buoyancy (upthrust)

# REAL WORLD SCIENCE

A submarine can change its density by taking in or pushing out water from special tanks. Submarines use **unbalanced forces** to move up or down through the water and balanced forces to hover in one place.

# What is Friction?

The **force** of gravity pulls you down a slide. But what makes you slow down and stop at the bottom?

The force that slows you down on a slide is called **friction**. Friction is a force between two things that are moving (or trying to move) across each other. Friction tries to stop the movement.

Friction only occurs when the two things touch each other. There is friction between the mat and the slide but not between the slide and the people (unless they touch the slide on their way down—ouch!).

There is friction between the wheels and the **axles** of a scooter. If you don't **balance** the friction with another push, the scooter will slow down and stop.

## Friction is Useful

Friction lets your foot grip the road when you push off it while riding a scooter, instead of sliding backwards. Friction means the wheels grip the road as they turn, so they travel across the road instead of spinning in one place. Friction between the wheel and the brake lets you slow down when you want to. Without friction, there would be no grip—and no scooting!

## SEE THE SCIENCE ↓

Friction produces heat. You can feel this when you rub your hands together. Try rubbing your hand back and forth across a smooth fabric, such as cotton, and a rough fabric, such as carpet. What do you notice?

# Rocket Racing

**Friction** is a **force** between two surfaces moving across each other. Does the type of surface change the amount of friction? This **experiment** will help you to find out.

## Equipment

- Balloons (long, thin ones are best)
- Masking tape
- Drinking straws
- 16-foot (5 m) lengths of wire or string with different textures (for example, wool, or nylon line)
- Clothespin
- Tape measure
- Marker

## Method

**1** Cut two 2-inch (5-centimeter) pieces of drinking straw, and thread them on to the first piece of string. Tie the string between two door handles or two pieces of furniture. Make sure the string is level and does not slope upwards or downwards.

**2** Blow up a balloon and close the neck with the clothespin. Tape the balloon to the straws as shown in the picture.

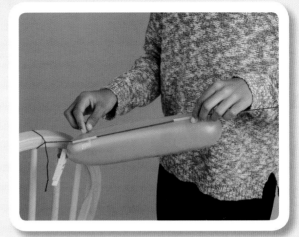

**3** Push the balloon rocket to the end of the string, and mark the starting position of the straw on the string.

**4** Unclip the clothespin and watch the balloon rocket zoom along. When it stops, mark the stopping position of the straw on the string. Measure the distance between the two marks, and record the result.

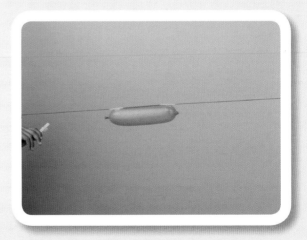

When the air rushes out of the balloon in one direction, it pushes the balloon in the other direction. A rocket works in the same way. The rocket pushes hot gases out downwards, and, in turn, these hot gases push the rocket upwards.

| Material | Distance traveled |
|---|---|
| Yarn | |
| Cotton thread | |
| Plastic wire | |
| Garden twine | |

Draw a table like this to record your results.

**Predict**: Will the balloon rocket travel the same distance along racetracks made from the other **materials**?

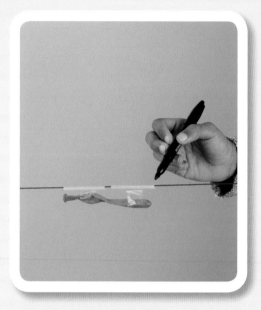

**5** Repeat steps 1 to 4 using each of the other racetrack materials. Use the same starting point and record the distance the rocket travels each time.

## IS IT A FAIR TEST?

To make it a fair test, you must start with the same amount of air in each balloon. Using a balloon pump can help you control how much air is put in. How could you make the test fair if you don't have a balloon pump? Is it a fair test if you use the same balloon each time? How could you improve your **experiment**?

**6** **Analyze** your results. Did the balloon rocket travel different distances along each track? Which **surfaces** helped the balloon travel farthest? Which surfaces slowed the balloon down more quickly?

## Conclusion

Balloon rockets travel further along smooth surfaces. There is more **friction** between rough surfaces than smooth surfaces. The friction between rougher surfaces slows things down more quickly.

## REAL WORLD SCIENCE

Smooth surfaces help to reduce friction. This is useful when we want to go fast. This ice slide is faster than a normal slide because the ice is very smooth. Can you think of any sports that use ice to reduce friction and make things go faster?

# Moving Through Air

Air resistance is a **force** that slows things down as they move through air. You can feel air resistance when you ride a bike. The faster you go, the harder it feels to push the air out of the way.

REAL WORLD SCIENCE

The only way to get rid of **friction** is to get rid of everything—even air! There is no air in space, so there is no air resistance to slow moving objects down. Once a spacecraft is traveling in space, the engines can be turned off and the spacecraft will keep going at the same speed forever. The space probe *Voyager 1* was launched in 1977 and is still whizzing through space now!

## Water Resistance

**Water resistance** is like air resistance, but it slows things down as they move through water. Smooth skin and a **streamlined** shape help sea animals to reduce water resistance and travel through the water more easily. Boats and submarines are designed the same way.

## SEE THE SCIENCE ⬎

Move your hand through water quickly. The pushing force you can feel is water resistance. Try moving spoons of different sizes through the water. What do you notice?

# Sail Boarding

Does the size of an object affect how it moves through air? Try this **experiment** to find out.

## Equipment

- Three identical toy cars or trains
- Three suckers
- Tape
- Three A4 sheets of thin cardboard

- Books
- Large sheet of thick cardboard (for example, the side of a cardboard box)
- Tape measure
- Large, smooth floor or table

## Method

1. Tape a sucker to each vehicle and add "sails" of different sizes:
   - A sheet of A4 card folded once
   - A sheet of A4 card folded twice
   - A sheet of A4 card folded three times

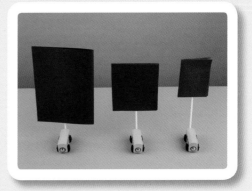

The weight of each car must be exactly the same, so use identical cars or add different sails to the same car. Make sure you use the same amount of card to make each sail, or the weight will be different, and it will not be a fair test.

**2** Set up a ramp using the books and cardboard. Position the ramp so there is enough space for the cars to roll down the ramp and across the table or floor.

**Predict**: Which car will travel the farthest when it rolls down the ramp and across the floor?

| Size of sail | Predicted rank | Distance traveled |
|---|---|---|
| ½ A4 | | |
| ¼ A4 | | |
| ⅛ A4 | | |

Draw a table like this to record your predictions and results.

**3** Hold the first car at the top of the ramp, then let go. When it comes to a stop, measure the distance between the end of the ramp and the back wheels. Record the result.

## ☑ IS IT A FAIR TEST?

A ramp is used to launch the cars, so that each car starts with the same forwards **force**. How else could you launch the cars, for a fair test?

**4** Repeat step three with the other cars. (Remember to move each car out of the way before you launch the next.) Each time, record the distance between the edge of the ramp and the back wheels.

**5** **Analyze** your results. Do they match your **prediction**?

## Conclusion

Did you find that the cars with smaller sails traveled farther? A smaller **surface area** means less **air resistance**. As a larger object moves through the air, it feels a bigger push in the **opposite** direction. This is why cars have **streamlined** shapes that reduce the surface area pushing air out of the way.

**REAL WORLD SCIENCE**

The streamlined shape of this jet plane helps it to move through the air more easily. When it's time to slow down, the large surface area of the parachute increases the air resistance quickly.

# Plan Your Next Experiment

**Experiments** have helped you discover some amazing things about **forces**. Just like you, scientists carry out experiments to answer questions and test ideas. Each experiment is planned carefully to make it a fair test.

Scientists are finding out new facts all the time. Experiments also lead to new questions!

Did you think of more questions about forces? Can you plan new experiments to help answer them?

Being a scientist and carrying out experiments is exciting. What will you discover next?

## YOU FOUND OUT THAT...

Forces are pushes or pulls. We need forces to make things move, stop moving, or change direction. When you push or pull an object, the object pushes or pulls back just as hard, in the **opposite** direction.

**Balanced** forces do not change the way an object moves. If an object is speeding up, slowing down, or changing direction. the forces on it must be **unbalanced**.

**Friction** is a force that slows moving objects down. There is more friction between rough surfaces than smooth surfaces.

**Air resistance** is a force felt by objects moving through air. **Water resistance** is a force felt by objects moving through water. Larger objects feel more air and water resistance than smaller objects.

## WHAT NEXT?

How could you change the speed at which the carton engine spins? Investigate what happens when you change the size of the holes.

A lump of play dough or modeling clay normally sinks. Can you make it float by changing its shape? Plan an experiment to find out.

How else could you help a balloon rocket to travel further? Plan an experiment to find out.

Plan an experiment to find out what size parachute you would need to carry a skydiving egg safely to the ground. Ask an adult to hard boil it first to avoid an eggy mess!

# Glossary

**air resistance** force that shows objects down as they move through air

**analyze** examine the results of an experiment carefully in order to explain what happened

**axle** rod that holds wheels in place

**balanced** forces that cancel each other out, so they have no overall effect

**buoyancy** upwards force on an object when it is put into liquid

**density** how heavy an object is for its size

**experiment** procedure carried out to test an idea or answer a question

**force** push or pull, which can make something start moving, stop moving, or change its shape

**friction** force that acts on objects moving over one another

**material** what something is made of

**observation** noting or measuring what you see, hear, smell, or feel

**opposite** completely different

**prediction** best guess or estimate of what will happen, based on what you already know

**scientific inquiry** method used by scientists to answer questions about the world

**streamlined** smooth and shaped to reduce air or water resistance

**surface area** total space on the outside of an object

**unbalanced** forces that do not cancel each other out, so together they cause an object to change speed, direction, or shape

**variable** something that can be changed during an experiment

**water resistance** force that slows objects down as they move through water

# Find out more

## Books

Biskup, Agnieszka. *Super Cool Forces and Motion Activities With Max Axiom*. Max Axiom Science and Engineering Activities. North Mankato, Minn.: Capstone Press, 2015.

Royston, Angela. *Forces and Motion*. Essential Physical Science. Chicago: Capstone Heinemann Library, 2014.

Weakland, Mark. *Thud!: Wile E. Coyote Experiments With Forces and Motion*. Wile E. Coyote, Physical Science Genius. North Mankato, Minn.: Capstone Press, 2014.

## Websites

FactHound offers a safe, fun way to find Internet sites related to this book. All of the sites on FactHound have been researched by our staff.

Here's all you do:

Visit *www.facthound.com*

Type in this code: 9781410979216

# Index